CANADA'S MAPLE LEAF

THE STORY OF OUR FLAG

written by

ANN-MAUREEN OWENS
& JANE YEALLAND

illustrated by

BILL SLAVIN
& ESPERANÇA MELO

Kids Can Press

For our parents
Larry and Mildred Brown — AMO
Jack and Joan Breadner — JY

Acknowledgements

Many thanks to the Honourable Judge John Matheson for his time, encouragement and interest in this project, as well as to Joan O'Malley and her father, Ken Donovan, for sharing their memories of the first Maple Leaf flag with us. Thanks also to Kevin Harrington of the Canadian Flag Association, the archivists at both the National Archives of Canada and Queen's University, and the staff at the Department of Canadian Heritage.

A big thank you to the students at St. Martha Catholic School, Kingston for testing the activities.
Thanks to both of our families for their continued patience and support with our deadlines.

Bill Slavin and Esperança Melo's beautiful illustrations helped bring the story of the flag to life.
It was again a pleasure to work with our fine editor, Liz MacLeod. Thanks to all the staff at Kids Can Press, especially book designer Julia Naimska and publishers Ricky Englander and Valerie Hussey.

Kids Can Press acknowledges the financial support of the Ontario Arts Council, the Canada Council for the Arts and the Government of Canada, through the BPIDP, for our publishing activity.

Flags are reproduced with the kind permission of the Department of Canadian Heritage, Protocol and Events Branch; Office of the Secretary to the Governor General; British Columbia Ministry of Finance and Corporate Relations; Government of Alberta; Saskatchewan Provincial Secretary; Manitoba Culture, Heritage and Citizenship; Government of Ontario; Province of New Brunswick; Communications Nova Scotia; Clerk of the Executive Council, Province of Prince Edward Island; Government of Newfoundland and Labrador; Legislative Assembly of the Northwest Territories; Government of Yukon.

Published in Canada by
Kids Can Press Ltd.
29 Birch Avenue
Toronto, ON M4V 1E2

Published in the U.S. by
Kids Can Press Ltd.
4500 Witmer Estates
Niagara Falls, NY 14305-1386

Edited by Elizabeth MacLeod
Designed by Julia Naimska
Printed in Hong Kong by Wing King Tong Co. Ltd.

CM   99 0 9 8 7 6 5 4 3 2 1
CM PA   99 0 9 8 7 6 5 4 3 2

Canadian Cataloguing in Publication Data
Owens, Ann-Maureen
    Canada's Maple Leaf: the story of our flag

Includes index.
ISBN 1-55074-459-3 (bound)   ISBN 1-55074-516-6 (pbk.)

1. Flags – Canada – Juvenile Literature. 1. Yealland, Jane.
II. Slavin, Bill. III. Melo, Esperança. IV. Title.

CR115.C2093 1999   929.9'2'0971   C98-931862-1

Kids Can Press is a Nelvana company

CONTENTS

CANADA'S UNIQUE FLAG

What do you think of when you see the Canadian flag? To most Canadians it means, "This is my country and I am proud of it." In this book you will find out how the Maple Leaf flag became Canada's national flag, why it is red and white, who made the first Canadian flag and much more.

Canada is the only country in the world with a maple leaf on its flag. That makes it unique in the world of flags.

Here are some flags of other nations that are also one-of-a-kind.

Like Canada, most countries have rectangular flags that are longer than they are high. But Switzerland's flag is square because it dates from the 1300s when that was a common flag shape.

The two pointed tails of Nepal's flag represent the peaks of the Himalayas, the highest mountains in the world. This flag started out as two triangular flags, one on top of the other.

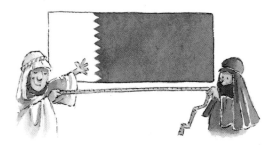

The longest national flag is Qatar's, a Middle Eastern country. Many flags are about twice as long as they are wide, but this flag is almost three times as long. Under the sun's rays, the flag's original red became maroon. Qatar made the colour change official to avoid confusion with the red flag of nearby Bahrain.

Libya is the only country with a single-coloured flag. Green is a sacred colour in the country's national religion, Islam.

The star is the most common emblem on national flags. But no flag has as many stars as the "Stars and Stripes" of the United States of America. This flag started with 13 stars in 1776 to represent the first 13 states, but a star was added for each new state and now there are 50.

Legend has it that Austria's flag dates from 1191 when Duke Leopold V took off his white tunic during battle and raised it on a stick to encourage his troops. The battle was so fierce that only the middle of the tunic, covered by Leopold's belt, remained white, while the rest became blood red.

BEFORE FLAGS

Flags have been used for thousands of years, but no one knows exactly who first made or used them. The first flags were made from wood and metal and were displayed from the tops of poles the same way flags are today. These solid flags, called vexilloids, were the beginning of today's flags.

Archeologists have discovered many vexilloids in China and Egypt that are more than 4000 years old. Some of these vexilloids are carved shapes such as a trident, which represents Neptune, the Greek god of the sea, or an eagle, which is a symbol of the Roman army.

Knights of England and France used symbols that told of their family background to decorate their shields and sometimes made vexilloids by mounting the shields on poles.

The change to fabric flags began when brightly coloured strips of cloth were tied to vexilloids to make them more noticeable. The first to do this were the Chinese, who made vexilloids in the shapes of fans and windsocks.

The Romans decorated their vexilloids by adding a crossbar and hanging cloth banners from it, and European knights transferred their shield designs onto square pieces of cloth. People quickly found that cloth emblems were easier to carry and more visible.

Vexilloids were also used by Canada's Aboriginal people. In 1577 explorer Martin Frobisher wrote in his diary that he had seen Inuit signalling to him with dried animal bladders tied to the tops of sticks.

The Plains Cree tied eagle feathers, which symbolize bravery, to the tops of poles that were wrapped in coloured strips of cloth. These feather poles were carried in ceremonies by the chiefs.

THE RAVEN

One of the first flags to fly in Canada arrived with the Vikings in the tenth century. When these Danish explorers landed on the shores of Newfoundland, they were probably carrying a triangular flag called "The Raven, Terror of the Land."

According to one legend, if the flag waved in the wind, making the raven appear to come to life, then the Vikings would win the battle.

FIRST FLAGS OVER CANADA

After the Vikings, explorers from countries such as France, England, Spain and Russia came to Canada and planted flags claiming land for their countries. Later, groups within Canada, such as the Métis and the Acadians, created their own flags.

British Columbia
- The Russian Naval Ensign was flown at various points on B.C.'s coast by explorers and fur traders from 1741 to 1784. This flag recently has been readopted as Russia's national flag.

- The Royal Arms of Spain was planted at Nootka Sound in 1789 when the Spanish seized two British ships. This almost led to war, but after five years of negotiation Spain finally lowered its flag and gave up all claims to B.C.

Alberta
- The "Stars and Stripes" was flown over some American trading forts that operated illegally in Alberta until the Mounties arrived to shut them down.

Manitoba
- By the early 1800s the Hudson's Bay Company had received permission from Britain to fly this flag from its ships and at its forts.

- This is Louis Riel's Red River Rebellion Flag of 1870. He hoped to talk Canada out of taking over Métis territory, but turned to rebellion when talks with the government failed. Métis hunters flew a similar flag to signal the start of the buffalo hunt.

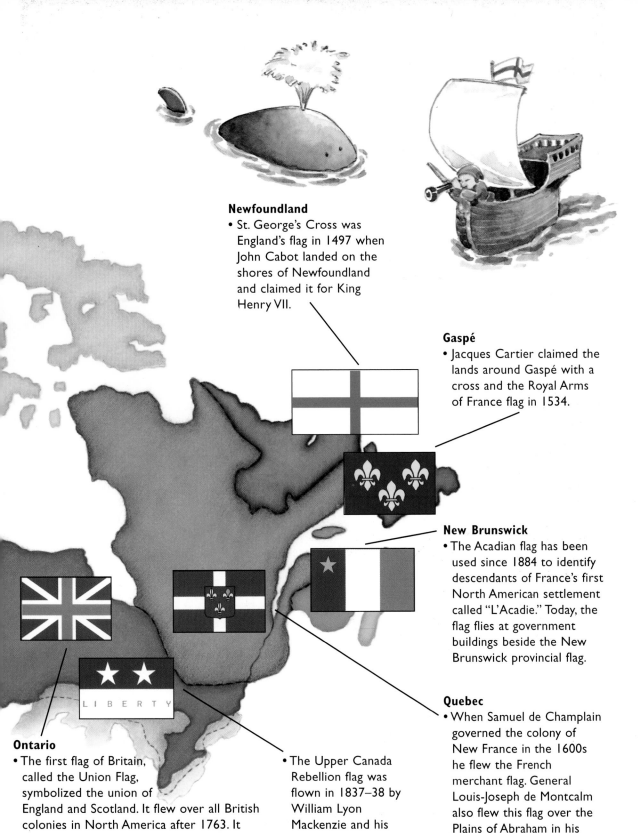

Newfoundland
- St. George's Cross was England's flag in 1497 when John Cabot landed on the shores of Newfoundland and claimed it for King Henry VII.

Gaspé
- Jacques Cartier claimed the lands around Gaspé with a cross and the Royal Arms of France flag in 1534.

New Brunswick
- The Acadian flag has been used since 1884 to identify descendants of France's first North American settlement called "L'Acadie." Today, the flag flies at government buildings beside the New Brunswick provincial flag.

Quebec
- When Samuel de Champlain governed the colony of New France in the 1600s he flew the French merchant flag. General Louis-Joseph de Montcalm also flew this flag over the Plains of Abraham in his 1759 battle with Britain's General James Wolfe.

Ontario
- The first flag of Britain, called the Union Flag, symbolized the union of England and Scotland. It flew over all British colonies in North America after 1763. It was also called the "Loyalists' Flag" because after the American revolution in 1776, it was carried north to Canada by those colonists who remained loyal to Britain.

- The Upper Canada Rebellion flag was flown in 1837–38 by William Lyon Mackenzie and his followers who wanted Canada to become a republic, independent of Britain.

LOYAL TO THE BRITISH FLAG

On July 1, 1867, Canada became a new country. It was called the Dominion of Canada and it included New Brunswick, Nova Scotia, Upper Canada (Ontario) and Lower Canada (Quebec). Across these provinces families and friends gathered to share picnic suppers. Later, as darkness fell, they celebrated their new country with fireworks and bonfires.

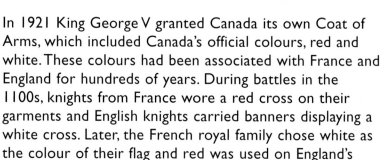

The flag flying across the new country was the Union Jack, Britain's national flag and a symbol of Canada's link with Britain. Canadians continued to fly the Union Jack for many years and Canadian soldiers fought under this flag during World War I.

In 1921 King George V granted Canada its own Coat of Arms, which included Canada's official colours, red and white. These colours had been associated with France and England for hundreds of years. During battles in the 1100s, knights from France wore a red cross on their garments and English knights carried banners displaying a white cross. Later, the French royal family chose white as the colour of their flag and red was used on England's royal flag.

The new Canadian Coat of Arms was added to the Red Ensign, a flag flown by Canadian ships. Canadian soldiers fought under this flag in World War II. At the end of the war in 1945, Parliament approved the flying of the Canadian Red Ensign on all government buildings until the country had a flag of its own. Usually, the Union Jack still flew beside the Canadian Red Ensign.

JACKS AND ENSIGNS

Jacks and ensigns are types of flags that countries fly on ships. The jack flies at the bow, or front, of a ship and tells you the ship's nationality. The ensign flies at the stern, or back, and tells you what kind of work the ship does. For example, the Red Ensign is the flag of British merchant ships, the White Ensign is flown by Royal Navy ships and the Blue Ensign is flown by any ship on government business. The legendary ship *Titanic* hoisted the Blue Ensign on her first and only voyage in 1912.

Unlike other countries, Britain uses one flag, the Union Jack, as both its national flag and its jack. Until Canada had its own flag, it flew the Red Ensign at sea and later flew a flag displaying Canadian symbols on land. Today, the provincial flags for Ontario and Manitoba are versions of the Canadian Red Ensign.

A FLAG OF CANADA'S OWN

Shouldn't a country have a flag of its own? This question was asked by the Canadian government after World War I and again after World War II. Many Canadians felt it was time for the country to choose a flag that would show Canada had a unique identity and was separate from Britain. This feeling became especially strong as Canada's 100th birthday approached. So members of all political parties vowed to work together to create a new flag for Canada.

In 1964, with Canada's 100th birthday only three years away, Prime Minister Pearson decided it was time once and for all for Canada to have its own flag. He organized a flag committee made up of 15 members of Parliament from the five political parties represented in the House of Commons. The committee's job was to find a flag design that would appeal to all Canadians.

As well as getting advice from flag experts, the flag committee asked Canadians for their suggestions. Thousands of people sent in ideas. The flag committee room was soon filled with bags and bags of mail containing letters and drawings from across Canada, and even from Canadians living outside the country.

Schoolchildren, families, homemakers, business people and organizations sent in drawings, paintings, collages and photographs, on tissue, wrapping paper, cardboard and fabric. Even a 100 kg (220 lb.) flag model with blinking lights was sent in. As members of the committee chose their favourite designs, they stuck them on the walls of the committee room. Soon the room was covered with hundreds of designs.

LESTER BOWLES (MIKE) PEARSON

Prime Minister Lester Pearson is remembered for much more than his fight to give Canada its own flag. Before becoming PM, Pearson had been president of the United Nations General Assembly. And in 1957 he won one of the world's highest honours, the Nobel Peace Prize, for his suggestion that the United Nations form a peacekeeping force to protect the world from war.

As well as being a world leader, Pearson had been a star athlete. He played semi-pro baseball and, while attending Oxford University in England, was on Britain's Olympic hockey team.

Every letter and flag design that was sent in to the government was delivered to the flag committee for consideration. People felt strongly about the need for a new flag, and most encouraged Prime Minister Pearson with his mission.

During his five years as prime minister (1963–68) Pearson gave Canada its pension plan and universal health care — as well as the country's new flag. He was passionate about Canada and its need for a flag. "I believe we should have a national flag that stands for Canada," said Pearson, "a flag that will say one word and that word is Canada."

Even though his favourite design — nicknamed the "Pearson Pennant," it had three red maple leafs on a white centre bordered by blue stripes — was not chosen as Canada's official flag, Pearson was proud to have helped Canadians get a flag as beautiful and unique as their country.

THOUSANDS OF FLAGS

What flag design would you have sent in? By far, the majority of designs involved a maple leaf. Some showed 12 leaves to represent the provinces and territories, and many colours were used besides red. The beaver, Mounties on horseback, religious symbols and the buffalo were some of the other suggestions.

Famous artists, such as the Group of Seven's A.Y. Jackson, sent in sketches and even spoke to the flag committee.

Some symbols were unusual, including rabbits, eagles, Canada geese and even hockey sticks. Often people sent in detailed letters explaining the meaning of their designs. Others mailed in poems, songs and even essays they had written in support of their ideas.

Today, thousands of those submissions, ranging from simple crayon sketches to professional artists' paintings, are saved at the National Archives of Canada as part of Canada's heritage.

THE MAPLE LEAF

Most of the designs people sent in for our national flag featured maple leaves. That's not surprising because maple trees grow across the country and the maple leaf had been a well-known symbol of Canada for a long time.

Maple trees were first used by Aboriginal people, who showed the settlers from Europe how to make maple syrup. In the 1800s residents of Lower Canada (Quebec) and Upper Canada (Ontario) decorated their homes and clothing with real maple leaves to welcome important visitors, such as the Prince of Wales from England.

The maple leaf has been embroidered or silk-screened on the athletic clothing of Canadian Olympic teams since 1904. It has also been used on Canadian soldiers' uniforms and gravestones as a symbol of their nationality since World War I.

THE GREAT FLAG DEBATE

After weeks of looking at designs and listening to experts, the flag committee had to choose a design to present to Parliament for approval. First the committee divided its favourite designs into three groups: versions of the Red Ensign, flags with a single maple leaf and ones with a number of maple leaves. Then the committee had to choose one of these groups.

Most of the suggestions in the multi-leaf category had three leaves.

Flag designs based on the Red Ensign also used the fleur-de-lis or other symbols.

Designs with a single maple leaf came in many colours and with or without borders.

The committee members were from five different political parties, so imagine how surprised they were when the votes were counted and they had all chosen the same category — the single maple leaf.

The flag committee presented its choice to Parliament. Now all members of Parliament had to vote on whether to approve this design as Canada's new flag. Getting them to agree would not be easy.

Prime Minister Pearson wanted a flag that was "distinctly Canadian which could not be mistaken for the emblem of any other country." He appealed to the honourable members to unite around the new flag.

But John Diefenbaker, leader of the Opposition, fought hard to keep the Red Ensign that showed Canada's historic link to Britain. Discussion led to debate that lasted for 15 days. It was one of the longest debates in the history of Canadian Parliament! The public galleries were jam-packed with people.

At 2:13 A.M. on December 15, 1964, debate was closed — something that is rarely done — and a vote was taken. Cheers, screams and desk-banging greeted the announcement that the Maple Leaf flag had received an overwhelming majority of votes from the members of Parliament.

Three days later the Senate passed the flag motion, and on December 31, Queen Elizabeth II, Canada's queen, gave her approval. Now it was official — after almost a hundred years, Canada had its own flag.

JOAN O'MALLEY'S FLAG

Before the debate and final vote on the flag design took place, Prime Minister Pearson wanted to see how the Maple Leaf flag would look. So he sent a secret request to his staff. Could they quickly make samples of the flag so he could fly them at his cottage that weekend?

When Ken Donovan, a government employee, got this message late on Friday afternoon, he panicked. What could he do? Everyone had left for the day. Who could sew the flags? Suddenly he had an idea and he quickly picked up his phone. "Joan," he said urgently when his 20-year-old daughter answered, "I need your help! Grab your sewing machine! You're going to sew Canada's new flag!"

It was already dark when Joan O'Malley, carrying her small sewing machine, met her father at a warehouse in downtown Ottawa. He hurried her inside and handed her metres and metres of red and white bunting that had to be sewn together and have all its edges hemmed. Joan had never tackled such a large sewing project before. Could she do it? Could she complete the flags by the deadline?

Joan set up her sewing machine and got to work. The machine whirred as she worked through the evening. Then she spent hours sewing by hand the hoist end where the toggle would go. It was after midnight when an exhausted Joan finished the job.

There was no time to waste! Joan's father leapt into his car and, escorted by the RCMP, sped to the prime minister's official home at 24 Sussex Drive. Joan wearily, but proudly, made her way home. She had sewed Canada's first flag.

Both Ken and Joan were instructed not to tell anyone of this late night adventure, and for many years they kept it secret. Joan, now with children and grandchildren of her own, still has that famous sewing machine.

"Back then I didn't really think of myself as playing a part in Canada's history," Joan says. "Now, years later, when I look back on that adventure, I feel glad that I was able to do something for my country. I still use that sewing machine but have promised to give it to the Canadian Museum of Civilization someday."

FLAG DAY

One reason Canada's Maple Leaf flag is recognized all around the world is because of its great design. That design was the result of a lot of hard work by a number of experts.

George Stanley, a professor at Royal Military College in Kingston, Ontario, suggested a single maple leaf design in red and white because it could be seen clearly from a distance.

Once Parliament voted for the red-and-white Maple Leaf flag, flag committee member John Matheson

worked to perfect the design. Red borders were included to balance the bold central leaf and make the flag stand out. Then Matheson had to choose a maple leaf as a model for the flag's leaf. He wanted to pick one that most Canadians would recognize so he chose the sugar maple leaf.

If you look at a sugar maple leaf you'll see it has 23 points, but the leaf on the flag has only 11 points. That's because John Matheson tested a model flag in the National Research Laboratory wind tunnel in Ottawa to see how it would look when it blew in the wind. He noticed that as the wind speed increased, the maple leaf design was hard to see because points on the leaf seemed to multiply.

The design of the leaf on the flag was developed by designer Jacques St. Cyr. His 11-point leaf looks like a real maple leaf when the flag flies on a windy day.

Just as there are many maple leaf shapes, there are also many shades of red. A bright scarlet shade was chosen for Canada's flag so that it would be different from the lighter red of Britain's Union Jack and the darker red of the American flag.

Most Canadians got their first glimpse of the new flag on February 15, 1965. It was a cold, cloudy day in Ottawa, but people began to gather on Parliament Hill early in the morning to welcome Canada's new flag.

By noon, there were over 15 000 kids and adults standing in the snow. A choir of Ottawa schoolchildren sang "O Canada" and Governor General Vanier and Prime Minister Pearson gave speeches. They described how the Maple Leaf flag would soon symbolize Canada to all Canadians and to the rest of the world.

A few tears were shed as the Canadian Red Ensign was lowered. But the crowd cheered and the sun broke through the clouds as the new Maple Leaf flag reached the top of the flagpole for the first time. Today, that original flag hangs in the prime minister's office.

FLYING COLOURS

HOW TO MAKE A FLAG

Millions of flags are made in Canada every year. Here's how you can make your own Canadian flag. Remember that the flag must be twice as long as it is wide and that each red end of the flag should be half the size of the white mid-section.

To make a flag 40 cm (16 in.) long and 20 cm (8 in.) wide, you'll need:
- a piece of white fabric, 45 cm x 20 cm (18 in. x 8 in.)
- a red marker or red fabric paint
- a piece of string 40 cm (16 in.) long
- a small stick 6 cm (2¹/4 in.) long
- a ruler, white glue, a sheet of white paper, scissors, a pencil

1. Measuring from left to right on the white fabric, draw lines at sections of 5 cm (2 in.), 15 cm (6 in.) and 35 cm (14 in.), as shown. Trace over each line with red marker or red fabric paint and colour in the two sections that are 10 cm (4 in.) wide.

2. To make the maple leaf shape, trace the maple leaf on the inside front cover of this book onto the white paper and cut it out with scissors.

3. Centre the paper leaf on the white section of the fabric and outline the leaf with red marker or red fabric paint. Remove the paper leaf and colour in the leaf shape. When the painted sections are dry, turn the flag over and colour in the red sections on the other side.

4. Centre the string on the small strip of white fabric at the side of the flag, leaving 10 cm (4 in.) of string at both the top and the bottom of the flag. Fold the fabric strip over the string and glue it.

5. To make the flag's toggle, which helps to hold the flag in place, tie the top end of the string around the centre of the short stick and tie a loop in the end of the string at the bottom of the flag.

RAISING THE FLAG

To fly your new flag, you can make your own flagpole. You'll need:
- a 1 kg (2.2 lb.) coffee can (and lid), filled with sand
- a 1 cm (3/8 in.) wide dowel, bamboo cane or stick about 125 cm (50 in.) long
- 2 bulldog clips, each 5.5 cm (2 in.) wide
- a piece of string 3 m (9 ft.) long
- a small stick 6 cm (2 1/4 in.) long
- scissors

2. Clamp one bulldog clip near the top of your pole and the other near its bottom, just above the coffee can lid.

4. To fly the flag that you made on page 22, pass the flag's toggle through the loop of string on your flagpole and the flagpole's toggle through the loop of string hanging from the bottom of your flag.

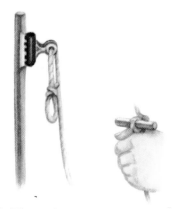

1. Using the tip of the scissors, poke a hole in the lid of the coffee can that is large enough to fit the dowel. Fit the lid on the can and push the dowel into the sand so it stands up on its own.

3. Thread the string through the holes of the top bulldog clip and tie a small loop to fit around the flag's toggle. At the other end of the string, tie on your small stick to make the flagpole's toggle.

5. Hoist the flag to the top of the pole and wind the string around the bulldog clip at the bottom of the pole to hold it in place.

MIND YOUR FLAG MANNERS

Unlike most countries, Canada has no laws about how its national flag is to be treated. It is just expected that it will be used with good manners and treated with respect. Here are some guidelines that the Canadian government suggests.

When Canada's Maple Leaf is flown with other flags or carried in a parade within Canada, it should be raised first and lowered last. The Canadian flag has the position of honour, so it should be the leading flag in a parade.

When there is a line of flags, the position of honour is either to the left of an observer or the middle position. A Canadian flag at each end of the line of flags is best, when this is possible.

Even without a flagpole, you can still hang your flag. Just make sure that the upper part of the leaf is pointing up and the stem is pointing down, or that the upper part of the leaf points left and the stem points right when seen by spectators.

On ships or boats, the Canadian flag should be displayed at the stern (back) when a Canadian boat is in harbour or in Canadian waters. Foreign ships may fly the Canadian flag as a "courtesy flag" at the bow or foremast (front). The only time you may fly the flag upside down is if you are in trouble and need help right away.

SPECIAL CANADIAN FLAGS

The only flags that can be flown above the national flag of Canada are the personal flags of the Queen and the governor general. Her Majesty's Personal Canadian Flag takes precedence over all flags in Canada whenever the Queen is visiting. It is usually used to show that the Queen is in residence or that she is attending a public ceremony.

When someone dies, flags can be flown at half-mast as a sign of mourning. First raise the flag to the top of the pole and then slowly lower it to a position approximately halfway down the pole.

This custom is based on the idea that in times of war, the flag of the victor is raised to the top of the pole. By flying a flag only at half-mast, room is being left at the top of the pole for the flag of the victor; in this case, the victor is death.

You can fly your flag at night as well as during the day. The important thing to remember is that it should not be flown when it becomes tattered or faded. If this happens, ask an adult to help you destroy your worn-out flag in a dignified way by burning it privately.

The governor general is the Queen's representative in Canada and so the governor general's Personal Flag flies above all flags except the Queen's flag. Like all personal flags, these flags can only be used by the people they represent.

SEND A FLAG MESSAGE

Signal flags are used at sea to send messages when ships can't communicate by radio. International code signal flags are used to spell out the words. During special celebrations, such as visits by royalty or Canada Day festivities, crews often "dress ship" by flying all the signal flags on board in colourful rows.

You can use the international code flags to send secret signals to a friend or to decorate your room with a coded message. You'll need:

- a 72 cm x 56 cm (29 in. x 22 in.) sheet of white bristol board
- coloured markers: red, black, yellow and medium blue
- scissors, a hole puncher, string

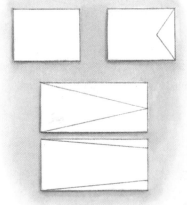

(Substitute flags are used when a letter is repeated in your message, and an answer flag shows that a response to a question is about to be given.)

1. Copy the designs of the 40 international code flags onto the white bristol board. Make an 8 cm x 6 cm (3 in. x 2 1/4 in.) flag for each letter. For the number, substitute and answer flags make 12 cm x 6 cm (4 3/4 in. x 2 1/4 in.) flags that taper to 4 cm (1 1/2 in.) or to a point, as shown.

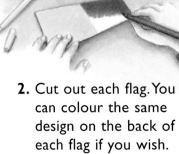

2. Cut out each flag. You can colour the same design on the back of each flag if you wish.

3. Punch two holes at the left side of each flag, as shown.

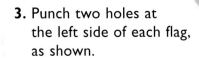

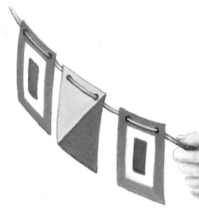

4. Arrange the flags to send your message from top to bottom or from left to right and thread a length of string through the punched holes, tying each flag in place if necessary.

5. Hang the flag signal for all to see, but give your friends a copy of the flag code so they can decipher your message.

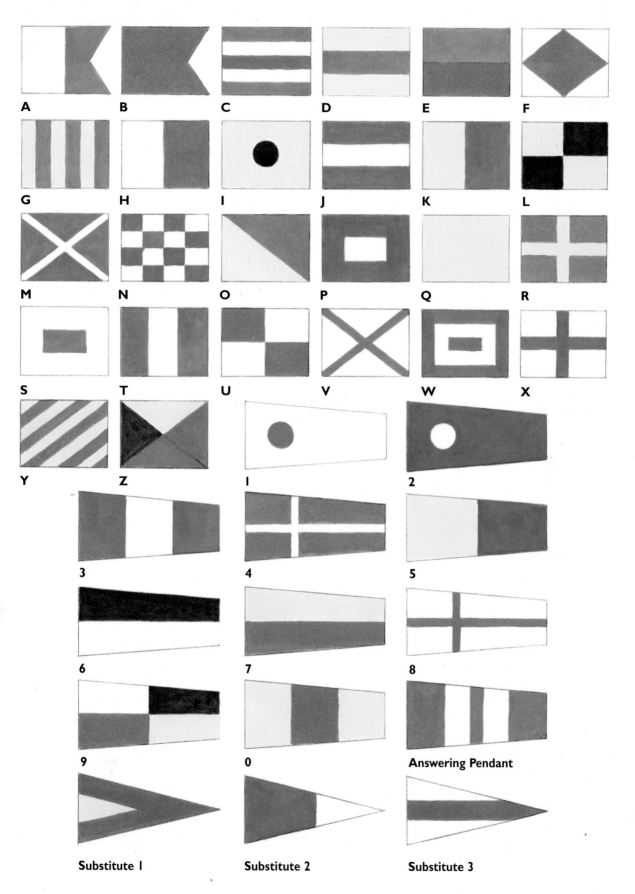

A B C D E F

G H I J K L

M N O P Q R

S T U V W X

Y Z 1 2

3 4 5

6 7 8

9 0 Answering Pendant

Substitute 1 Substitute 2 Substitute 3

PROVINCIAL FLAGS

Every province and territory in Canada has its own flag, and each one has a story to tell about its people and their part of the country.

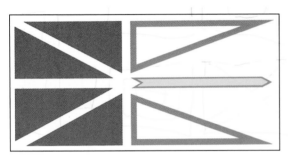

The newest provincial flag belongs to Newfoundland. It was created in 1980 and includes a golden arrow pointing the way to a bright future. The two red triangles stand for the island and mainland parts of the province, blue emphasizes Newfoundland's dependence on the sea and white symbolizes snow and ice.

Nova Scotia's flag is the oldest provincial flag. England's King Charles I made it official in 1625 when Nova Scotia was a British colony. Settlers from Scotland chose symbols from their homeland for their flag, such as the cross of St. Andrew (the patron saint of Scotland) and the Scottish lion.

Prince Edward Island's flag is easy to recognize because it has an island on it. The English lion comes from the coat of arms of the prince after whom the island was named. The large tree is the oak of England and the three saplings stand for the province's three counties: King's, Queen's and Prince.

The gold lion of England is also on New Brunswick's flag. The ship is from the crest of the Duke of Brunswick, who was King of England when the province was founded. This flag was made official in 1965, just nine days after Canada's national flag flew for the first time.

Quebec's flag shows its roots as a colony of France. The white cross on a blue background is from an ancient military banner that French knights carried as long ago as the twelfth century. The four fleurs-de-lis are also symbolic of France and give Quebec's flag its popular name of the "fleurdelisé" flag.

In 1966 Manitoba chose to use a red ensign with the provincial crest as its provincial flag. Manitoba's crest features the buffalo, which was so important to Aboriginal people. It also includes the cross of St. George of England to symbolize the province's ties with Britain and the Hudson's Bay Company.

Ontario adopted a flag that closely resembles the Canadian Red Ensign in 1965, a few months after the Red Ensign was replaced by Canada's national flag. The Union Jack in the upper left corner and the red cross of St. George on the crest both show the loyalty that Ontario's early settlers felt for Britain. The golden maple leaves stand for Canada.

In 1969 Saskatchewan held a provincial flag design competition. The winning design includes a background of green for the province's northern forests and gold for its southern wheat fields. The provincial shield and the provincial flower, the western red lily, are both on the flag.

During Canada's 100th birthday celebrations in 1967, Alberta began using this flag. It officially adopted it a year later. The flag's main feature is the shield granted to Alberta by King Edward VII in 1907. It shows mountains, foothills, prairies and grain fields under the British cross of St. George.

The Yukon Territory's flag was designed by a student who won a flag design contest during Canada's 100th birthday celebrations in 1967. The flag features the Yukon's special flower, the fireweed, and a malamute, the sled dog that provided the earliest form of transportation in the Yukon.

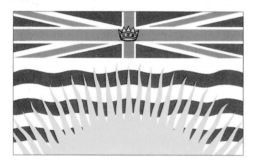

The design of British Columbia's flag is based on its shield, which was granted by King Edward VII in 1906. The Union Jack and crown symbolize the province's origin as a British colony. A golden setting sun and three wavy blue bars show B.C.'s location on Canada's west coast.

The Northwest Territories have used this flag since 1969 when it was chosen in a nationwide flag design contest. The flag has a wavy blue line to represent the Northwest Passage through the polar ice. The Arctic fox and the gold bars show the North's wealth.

In 1999 Nunavut became Canada's newest territory. The gold and blue of Nunavut's flag symbolize the riches of the land, sea, and sky, while the red refers to Canada. The traditional Inuit stone monument, the *inuksuk,* guides the people of the north as does the North Star.

FLAG PARTS & INTERNET LINKS

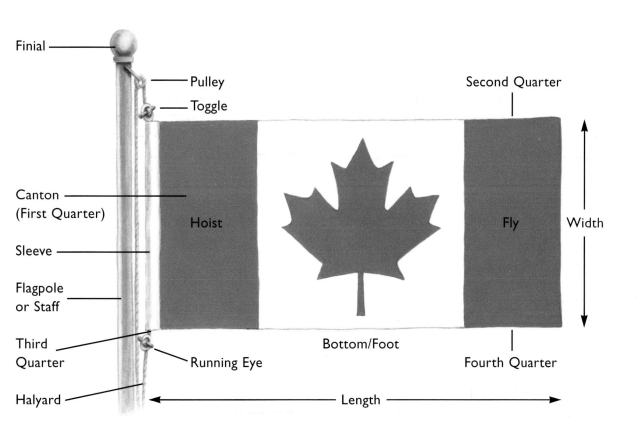

Finial

Pulley

Toggle

Second Quarter

Canton
(First Quarter)

Hoist

Fly

Width

Sleeve

Flagpole
or Staff

Third
Quarter

Running Eye

Bottom/Foot

Fourth Quarter

Halyard

Length

Check out these flag-friendly sites on the Internet:

Canadian Heritage: http://www.pch.gc.ca/ceremonial-symb/english.htm

The Flag Institute: http://www.flaginst.demon.co.uk/links.html

North American Vexillogical Association:
http://users.aol.com/Donh523/navapage/canada.htm

National Flags: http://www.anbg.gov.au/flags/nation-flags.html

International Marine Signal Flags:
http://www.anbg.gov.au/flags/signal-meaning.html

INDEX